Memorial Stones

A Guided Devotional Journal of
Foundational Miracles in Your Life

Brenda Savanhu

ISBN 979-8-89130-996-8 (paperback)
ISBN 979-8-89130-997-5 (digital)

Christian Faith Publishing
832 Park Avenue
Meadville, PA 16335
www.christianfaithpublishing.com

Printed in the United States of America

To Irene Savanhu, prayer warrior, Jesus lover, giant of the faith, and my mother.

It is because of you I've written this book. Little did I know what was being imparted to me as I observed how you lived your life. I will continue to run my race as you cheer me on from the great cloud of witnesses.

Love, Bee

CONTENTS

ABOUT THIS DEVOTIONAL JOURNAL

Hi there, miracle recipient!

Yes, you! I am talking to you! You have witnessed and received so many miracles in your life, and we are about to go on a journey to document twelve foundational miracles you can recall. I know you're thinking, *How on earth will I remember twelve foundational miracles I've witnessed?* Trust that the Holy Spirit will bring to remembrance what you need to document.

I believe this journey you are about to go on will be transformational in reminding you of what God has done in your life and set an unshakable foundation of faith that will always point you to His faithfulness, His *long* faithfulness! The faithfulness of God is long! It goes the distance!

Remembering the miracles He has done has always helped me navigate any challenging real-time circumstances. I remember He provided just enough when it looked like I didn't have enough. When I think I'm about to quit, I remember when He carried me. Remembering bolsters my faith and helps me to keep going. It reminds me my faith is not in vain. It helps to fix my gaze on Him during a bumpy ride.

This book is a guided devotional journal with specific questions that will cause you to pause and dig deep for answers. Each entry begins with the name of Jacob's sons, who make up the twelve tribes of Israel—each name with its meaning. The questions will ask you to recall a miracle in your life in relation to the meaning of each name. Once you have completed all twelve entries, plus two bonus entries, scan the QR code on page 61 to download worksheets where you can summarize and document each miracle and post them where you can easily see the miracles you recorded.

If you get to a particular memorial stone and cannot recall a miracle, move on to the next one. It could mean that you have not seen a miracle in that area yet. Be kind to yourself. You don't have to finish this in twelve consecutive days. As you recall, you may have to park at an entry for a few days, and perhaps some healing work needs to be done. There is an extra sheet you can make copies of and continue to document miracles, because the miracles didn't stop at twelve!

What do you think? Are you up for this journey? If so, I need you to make some room, get into a quiet space, light a candle, make yourself a cup of tea or coffee, get your cozy throw, and let's begin!

Blessings + miracles.

Brenda

INTRODUCTION

The biblical inspiration for this devotional came from the Book of Joshua. After Moses died, Joshua was appointed the new leader of the Israelites. God told Joshua to lead the Israelites across the Jordan River into the promised land.

Joshua received precise instructions about how this would happen. The Levitical priests would go ahead of the Israelites, carrying the ark of the covenant, and stand in the Jordan. The Lord said to Joshua He would take the land from the Canaanites, Hittites, Hivites, Perizzites, Girgashites, Amorites, and Jebusites when the ark of the covenant of the Lord of the whole earth would go ahead of the Israelites into the Jordan (Joshua 3:10–11 NASB).

The Jordan River was at flood stage, but as soon as the Levitical priests' feet touched the water, the river stopped flowing and rose into a mass, backing up as far as the city of Adam. The Israelites crossed on *dry ground*. Once the entire nation had crossed, the Lord told Joshua to get twelve men, one from each tribe, to take twelve stones from the middle of the Jordan where the Levitical priests were standing. They were to carry those stones to the place the Israelites would camp that night. The Lord told Joshua the following regarding the stones,

> This shall be a sign among you; when your children ask later, saying, "What do these stones mean to you?" Then you shall say to them, "That the waters of the Jordan were cut off before the ark of the covenant of the Lord; when it crossed the Jordan, the waters of the Jordan were cut off."

So these stones shall become a memorial to the
sons of Israel forever. (Joshua 4: 6–7 NASB)

I love this idea of memorial stones to remember what the Lord
has done. We may not have literally crossed the Jordan, but there
have been many Jordans we have had to cross to enter into our promised land. As I thought about this idea further, I thought about the
stories of Leah, Rachel, Bilhah, and Zilpah. They had borne the
tribes of Israel. Each son's name was an answer to prayer and had a
specific meaning. I thought we could explore how God has answered
prayers in our lives using the meanings of the names of the tribes
(sons) of Israel.

Prayer for You

I pray as you walk through this guided devotional journal,
you will be able to document some of the foundational miracles in
your life that continue to inform your journey today. I ask that God
would bring to memory the different times in your life these miracles
occurred. I pray that anywhere there is pain in remembering, God
would bring healing to those places. I pray that you will experience
miracles at the memorial stones where you have not seen a miracle
yet.

As you document and remember, may your faith walk grow
stronger, and may you be blessed in the wonder of it all. I pray that
these miracles not only impact you but that they may impact all
your descendants and future generations until the second coming of
Christ. May these be some of the miracles you will continue to share
as you remember the faithfulness of God in your life. In Jesus's name,
I pray. Amen.

BEFORE YOU BEGIN

Let's get some context for the portion of Jacob's life we use as the foundation for this journey.

> So when Laban heard the news about Jacob, his sister's son, he ran to meet him, and embraced him and kissed him, and brought him to his house. Then he told Laban all these things. And Laban said to him, "You certainly are my bone and my flesh." And he stayed with him a month. Then Laban said to Jacob, "Because you are my relative, should you therefore serve me for nothing? Tell me, what shall your wages be?" Now Laban had two daughters; the name of the older was Leah, and the name of the younger was Rachel. And Leah's eyes were weak, but Rachel was beautiful in figure and appearance. Now Jacob loved Rachel, so he said, "I will serve you seven years for your younger daughter Rachel." Laban said, "It is better that I give her to you than to give her to another man; stay with me." So Jacob served seven years for Rachel, and they seemed to him like *only* a few days because of his love for her. (Genesis 29:13–20 NASB)

Laban's Treachery

Then Jacob said to Laban, "Give *me* my wife, for my time is completed, that I may have relations with her." So Laban gathered all the people of the place and held a feast. Now in the evening he took his daughter Leah and brought her to him; and *Jacob* had relations with her. Laban also gave his female slave Zilpah to his daughter Leah as a slave. So it came about in the morning that, behold, it was Leah! And he said to Laban, "What is this *that* you have done to me? Was it not for Rachel that I served with you? Why then have you deceived me?" But Laban said, "It is not the practice in our place to marry off the younger before the firstborn. Complete the week of this one, and we will give you the other also for the service which you shall serve with me, for another seven years." Jacob did so and completed her week, and he gave him his daughter Rachel as his wife. Laban also gave his female slave Bilhah to his daughter Rachel as her slave. So *Jacob* had relations with Rachel also, and indeed he loved Rachel more than Leah, and he served with Laban for another seven years. (Genesis 29:21–30 NASB)

Jacob negotiated to work for Laban for seven years so he could marry Rachel. Consequently, he was deceived by Laban into marrying Leah before he could have Rachel. What drama! This was the place the tribes of Israel were birthed! In the midst of deceit!

Yet let's watch God show us how the birthing of the tribes of Israel ties into our lives' foundational miracles. Let's jump in!

Reuben—Has Seen My Affliction (Sounds Like)

Reuben was Jacob's firstborn, birthed by Leah, the sister Jacob was tricked into marrying. Leah knew Jacob did not love her and hoped that by giving him his first son, he would grow to love her.

> Now the Lord saw that Leah was unloved, and He opened her womb, but Rachel was unable to have children. Leah conceived and gave birth to a son, and named him Reuben, for she said, "Because the Lord has seen my affliction; surely now my husband will love me." (Genesis 29:31–32 NASB)

At age fifteen, the school secretary called me to the office. As I walked across campus toward the white stucco administrative building, the blooming jacaranda trees and the beautifully manicured grounds quickly faded into the background as my mind zeroed in on one thought: *Uh-oh. I'm in trouble!* As soon as the thought flew into my head, I found myself standing in the entryway in front of the massive wooden door with glass panels.

I took a deep breath and slowly turned the handle to open the door. I turned left and made my way to the secretary's office. Her desk loomed in front of me the closer and closer I stepped. She looked up as I came to a stop. I greeted her and told her my teacher sent me to the office. She asked for my name then ruffled through some papers and read a note.

She looked up again and said, "Your mother's office called. Go there as soon as the bell rings."

I thanked her as I did a cartwheel in my head. *Phew! I wasn't in trouble!* I only thought of the message once the school bell rang for the day. My friends and I would walk or ride the school van into the city center. On this day, we all climbed into the fifteen-passenger van. My mother's office directed me to get there ASAP, so this was perfect. Once the van dropped us off at city hall, we all bid each other farewell and scattered in different directions.

While hiking the two-block walk to Mum's office building, I began dreading the response of the invariably grouchy security guard at the check-in desk who always felt the need to interrogate me even though he knew me.

Surprisingly on this day, he just waved me through. That should have been my clue that something was very wrong. I waited for the elevator, stepped in when the doors opened, and braced myself for my stomach to flip as it whisked me to the seventh floor. I exited and walked to the reception desk.

Usually quite friendly, the receptionist looked at me concerned. I smiled and greeted her, and she asked me to sit down. She summoned my mother's coworkers. These maternal women surrounded me as the receptionist sat beside me and told me my mother had collapsed in the break room earlier. After seeing the look of horror on my face, she quickly said they had taken her to the doctor and that she was much better. They had called my school to leave me a message and brought her back to the office so I could accompany her home.

At that point, I still had not seen my mother, who was in her office resting. I stood up and left the reception area, and as I walked into her office, I saw my six-year-old brother there. He was sitting on the floor wearing his khaki school uniform, reading a book, oblivious to the world around him. *Someone must have brought him from school,* I thought.

I greeted my mother, looked her over, and asked what happened. As all mothers do, she tried to brush off my concern and said she was okay. In the meantime, her coworkers arranged for a driver to bring us home. Tears started pouring down my face as we squeezed into the car's back seat. I couldn't hold them back. I cried because the thought of losing my mother terrified me. My parents divorced a few years earlier; losing her would mean living with my father. During the demise of their marriage, my mother packed us up one morning in the middle of the week, and we left after my father attacked my sister. So the idea of living with him truly petrified me.

As I sat in the back of that car, and an endless stream of tears flowed, I was afflicted with the horrifying possibility that if we lost Mum, we would have to live with the father whom I was pretty sure did not love us. We could not lose her. I later learned my mother lost consciousness due to low blood sugar. Mum went on to live many beautiful years. I know that God saw my affliction and kept my mother well. Of that, I am sure.

Recall the very first time you remember the Lord *seeing* your affliction.

What was happening in your life at that time? How old were you?

What were you facing? Did the challenge feel insurmountable?

What was the affliction?

What sign did the Lord give you that He has seen your affliction?

MEMORIAL STONE 2

Simeon—Has Heard
(That I Am Unloved)

Leah also birthed Simeon, Jacob's second born. Giving Jacob his firstborn did not make him love Leah, so she realized Jacob would never love her.

> Then she conceived again and gave birth to
> a son, and said, "Because the LORD has heard that
> I am unloved, He has therefore given me this *son*
> also." So she named him Simeon. (Genesis 29:33
> NASB)

In Reuben, Memorial Stone 1, I mentioned that Mum packed us up one morning after my father attacked my sister. That was the beginning of their separation, which ultimately ended in divorce. I was twelve years old when we left. That morning, I went to school from the house my parents had made our home and went home to a completely different place in a different suburb in a single-parent household. This life change began a new journey that would significantly mark my life.

One Saturday morning, soon after we had moved out, Mum and I went into town to shop. I loved going places with Mum. I would always hop into the car even when she mildly protested and let me come with her anyway. I wore a burgundy ruffle skirt, a white tank top, and sandals that morning. When we arrived at Meikles Department Store, Mum parked her yellow Peugeot in a parking space in the middle of the street. The city I grew up in was famously known for incredibly wide streets, most of which had parking spaces in the middle of the road.

We got out of the car, and I took in Saturday morning's hustle and bustle in Bulawayo, Zimbabwe. Gosh, how I loved the city! Mum beckoned me to her, and she grabbed my left hand as we prepared to cross the street. One of the things she had always taught me was that even as she checked for oncoming traffic, I had to do the same along with her. That is when I saw him, my father, across the street. I said, "Mum, look, there's Dad."

As she looked up, he looked up and met both of our gazes. At that moment, I knew he would wait for us to cross, and ask me how I was doing. Friends, the unimaginable happened. Instead of waiting for us to cross the street, he turned around and walked away.

I was stunned! He didn't even wave—nothing! I looked at Mum, wide-eyed, and said incredulously, "He couldn't say hi?"

She pulled me in the other direction and said, "Brenda, I am not sure what you expected. That is your father." I was crushed. I knew my parents had their issues. I knew my father had violently attacked my sister, but I never thought that my father would choose to ignore me. I guess some small part of me was hoping for remorse and a move toward repentance, but that did not happen.

That day, that Saturday, was the day I felt unloved.

Mum didn't give me too much time to dwell on it. She whisked me away quickly into Meikles and refocused my attention on our shopping adventure. Being refocused was precisely what I needed at that time. It was what I needed to survive. It wasn't until years later that I dug back into that incident, and God healed me. I realized that the miracle at that time was focusing my attention in a different direction until I could process that rejection.

Can you recall a time in your life you felt unloved?

What was happening in your life at that time?

Did you realize that God heard your cry of being unloved at the time?

What sign did the Lord give you that He had heard you're unloved?

MEMORIAL STONE 3

Judah—I Will Praise the Lord

Leah realized Jacob would never love her, yet she became pregnant again and gave birth to Judah. The name *Judah* means "praise"! I love how Leah grew into a place of praise even after realizing her husband could not love her, nor could she earn his love. I'm sure both realizations crushed her spirit and devastated her personally, but she still found the strength to praise the Lord.

> And she conceived again and gave birth to a son, and said, "This time I will praise the LORD." Therefore she named him Judah. Then she stopped having children. (Genesis 29:35 NASB)

I took the day off work on Friday, July 6, 2007, because I had a 10:00 a.m. life-changing appointment. I woke up that morning and went through my day-off routine: I did my forty-five-minute DVD workout, showered, made myself some eggs and oatmeal for breakfast, and then it was time to get dressed. My chosen outfit had been laundered, ironed, and hung the night before. It was ready to be worn.

I recently went shopping and found a double-layered cotton black flowy knee-length skirt, a soft ivory cotton-wrap blouse, and a pair of strappy ivory open-toe heels. After getting dressed, it was time to document the occasion with pictures. My sister and roommate took pictures of me outside, and then it was time to go.

As l drove to my appointment, I took in the day's beauty. It was a beautiful summer day. The day's beauty helped ease my apprehension as I got closer to my destination. After I arrived, I parked my car, took a deep breath, and made my way up the steps to the glass doors and into the courthouse. Today was the day of the hearing for my divorce.

Several factors led to my marriage's demise that will take too long to detail here. I will share that in the unraveling of our marriage, I saw the gradual loss of my identity. In my excitement to be a good wife, I went my way without God, which led to losing my Christ-centered identity, as I constantly accommodated my husband's dreams in my strength. I had pushed God out for six years while slowly chipping away at my identity. Unfortunately, our marriage came to an end. I decided to return to my faith-based roots as I reviewed my life at this new juncture. I recommitted myself and my life to Jesus Christ because I had indeed made a mess out of my life without Him.

You might be wondering why on earth I would choose to record the day of my divorce as a praiseworthy miracle. When I got to this memorial stone, I asked the Lord to give me a picture of the first time I praised without lament or expectation. He showed me the picture of me on the porch wearing the outfit I described. Secondly, praise was the immediate response because I was the prodigal returning home to the arms of my loving Father.

Now that I had returned home, He began to take me on a journey of who He created me to be. A journey I am still on today. A journey that started in the demise of one relationship but reignited the flame in another.

If you have been through a divorce, you know the decision is not easy, but I pray that you find healing and redemption in your relationship with the Father.

Recall a time you praised the Lord without lament or expectation.

What was happening in your life at that time?

Why was praise the immediate response this time?

What did the Lord do for you that caused you to praise?

MEMORIAL STONE 4

Dan—God Has Vindicated Me

Leah gave birth to three healthy boys which, in biblical times, was a tremendous accomplishment. In those days, giving birth to a male meant grater power and glory for the tribe. Rachel, however, suffered from a "closed womb," and her jealousy of her sister consumed her. In her desperation, she decided to give her maid, Bilhah, to Jacob to hopefully conceive a surrogate son.

> Now when Rachel saw that she had not borne Jacob *any* children, she became jealous of her sister; and she said to Jacob, "Give me children, or else I am going to die." Then Jacob's anger burned against Rachel, and he said, "Am I in the place of God, who has withheld from you the fruit of the womb?" Then she said, "Here is my female slave Bilhah: have relations with her that she may give birth on my knees, so that by her I too may obtain a child." So she gave him her slave Bilhah as a wife, and Jacob had relations with her. Bilhah conceived and bore Jacob a son. Then Rachel said, "God has vindicated me, and has indeed heard my voice and has given me a son." Therefore she named him Dan. (Genesis 30:1–6)

In January 2015, I started the year feeling restless. Not in a bad way, but the kind of restlessness you feel in anticipation of a new season. Looking back on my sporadic journaling, part of an entry on January 25, 2015, reads, "You have a divine purpose for me. A calling upon my life, so here I am, Lord. Send me." Had I known what that "sending" would look like, I'm not sure I would have prayed that prayer.

Soon after, I was asked by my boss if I would be interested in transferring to a new city under a team he would be leading to open a new property. I took that inquiry to my prayer closet and felt the peace to proceed with a yes. When I returned to my boss with my answer, knowing I had his support, I knew this transfer process would be a shoo-in. How wrong I was.

Initially, I received a tentative yes. The yes came with conditional stipulations ensuring I continued to do a good job, which I knew would not be an issue because I was a good worker. My boss soon left for the new city to get things started. Someone else replaced him, who quickly told me on their third day on the property that I was doing a terrible job and would not be transferring. I responded immediately by presenting evidence to the contrary, but as you can imagine, our relationship got off on the wrong foot. Despite the evidence, the decision that I could not go remained.

Several weeks later, I was told it was a go again. I could transfer. But first, I had to meet with the regional vice president to get my final yes. I would meet with him during his scheduled property visit. On the day and time I was to meet with him, I was diverted by my new boss, who sat me down and told me the meeting would not be happening; therefore, I would not be transferring.

I was livid. I felt like a tennis ball being volleyed continuously over the net. Our exchange was less than cordial, and I was feeling dejected. One thing I knew for sure after that meeting was I needed guidance. I had to attend my church's weekly Tuesday night prayer service. God answered my prayer for guidance using 2 Chronicles 20:15(NASB):

And he said, "Listen, all *you* of Judah and the
inhabitants of Jerusalem, and King Jehoshaphat:

> This is what the LORD says to you: 'Do not fear
> or be dismayed because of this great multitude,
> for the battle is not yours but God's.'" (2 Chron-
> icles 20:15 NASB)

At that moment, I gave up fighting. I still wasn't happy, but I knew the battle was not mine. By now, we were at the end of March, so it had been a little over two months. What I thought would be a simple process turned out to be one of the most frustrating experiences of my life.

I still felt the restlessness from January and kept asking the Lord where I needed to go because I knew my time was up there. The conversation came up again; once again, it was a possibility that I would go. Honestly, by this time, I was tired of drinking the Kool-Aid and really did not believe it. But I knew that God could do the impossible, so I brought the prayer up to Him again.

It was the Tuesday after Memorial Day, 2015, and I was off to the Tuesday night prayer meeting. As I made my way to church that evening, I was wrestling with being emotionally and mentally tired of the last five months regarding my transfer. That evening, the message was based on Revelation 3:7-8 (NASB):

> And to the angel of the church in Philadel-
> phia write:
> He who is holy, who is true, who has the
> key of David, who opens and no one will shut,
> and who shuts and no one opens, says this:
> I know your deeds. Behold, I have put
> before you an open door which no one can shut,
> because you have a little power, and have fol-
> lowed My word, and have not denied My name.
> (Revelation 3:7–8 NASB)

My pastor said, "Just because you're weak doesn't mean that God cannot break open a door."

There was an altar call, and I couldn't make it there fast enough. With everything in me, I cried out to the Lord, "Please either open the door or close it because I am tired." My friend Shelly made her way to me and prayed for me. I don't recall what she prayed, but I know I felt it in the depths of my soul.

I was summoned to the general manager's office on Thursday of that week. I didn't know why I had been called to his office, nor did I speculate. He asked me to sit down, looked at me, and said, "You're going to Houston."

I responded with a blank stare. He asked me what I thought, and I told him, "You all have been yanking me around, so forgive me if I don't believe you." Then he gave me a signed letter with the transfer approval. I looked at it to confirm, and then I allowed myself a smile. As I exited his office with the letter securely in my hand, I gave God praise! After five months of battle, the Lord had vindicated me!

Recall a time you received an answer to prayer as vindication from the Lord.

What was happening in your life at that time? What was the Lord vindicating you from?

What was this blessing the Lord gave you that you received as vindication? Why did you receive it as vindication?

MEMORIAL STONE 5

Naphtali—To Wrestle

After Bilhah conceives a second time, Rachel feels like she is finally beating her sister in this competition of giving Jacob sons and determines that she has triumphed in this wrestling with her sister.

> And Rachel's slave Bilhah conceived again and bore Jacob a second son. So Rachel said, "*With* mighty wrestling I have wrestled with my sister, *and* I have indeed prevailed." And she named him Naphtali. (Genesis 30:7–8 NASB)

After transferring into the previously mentioned job in Dan, Memorial Stone 4, I felt burned-out six months into the job. But I'll save the gory details of that story for another day. Oh yeah, you heard right. I sure did get burned-out in a job I know God sent me into.

By the time the ball dropped on January 1, 2016, I knew something needed to change. I cried out to God day and night to show me what to do, whether to leave the job or if He could download a strategy to mitigate this torturous burnout. Month after month, I prayed without any definitive answer.

Then in July 2016, I got incredibly sick at work and had to go home in the middle of the day. The next day, I went to see my doctor, who ran some tests that revealed I was iron-deficient anemic. She referred me to an OB-GYN because the iron loss was due to heavy monthly blood losses. My OB-GYN quickly recommended surgery to remove the fibroids causing this serious blood loss. For anyone who has been iron-deficit anemic, you know that fatigue is one of the symptoms, which in my case was exacerbated by working sixteen- to eighteen-hour days.

Surgery was scheduled two months later for mid-September. I submitted my medical leave paperwork and left with the anticipation of returning after my four-week recovery period. As the time neared for me to return to work, I felt God wanted me to leave my job. I decided to fast and pray for clarity on what I thought I was hearing. "Three days would do it," I told myself.

Apparently, I overestimated. I received the answer at the end of my first day of fasting. Truthfully, I believed the answer came too quickly for me, so I continued to fast for the next two days. I'm not sure if I needed to make sure I heard correctly or if I really wanted to procrastinate. In my heart, I knew I needed to resign. This was one of the most difficult decisions I have ever made. Trusting God with your career, your livelihood, and your income is almost overpoweringly difficult. You would think this wrestling—the wrestling to quit my job—would be enough, but it wasn't.

More wrestling came after I left my job. I was intent on job hunting because I had bills to pay, but the Lord kept telling me to rest. This went against everything I knew. How could I rest when I did not have an income? To me, not looking for work was lazy and dishonoring of God. But in this instance, He told me that I needed to rest in Him and that resting rather than working was the "work" I needed to do. Would I have faith and trust that He would take care of me and ensure all of my needs were met? I struggled with the scripture that faith without works is dead (James 2:6), but He had to reveal to me that in this case, and for my particular situation, "works" was learning to trust Him to take care of me without going to look for work.

The triumph in this wrestling was, I learned a new perspective. As I rested, God provided for all of my needs. I did not go to bed hungry or lose the roof over my head. He was faithful to provide for me so that I could rest.

Recall a time you remember wrestling for an answer to prayer.

What was happening in your life at that time?

Who or what were you wrestling for that answer?

How did the Lord answer that prayer you wrestled over?

MEMORIAL STONE 6

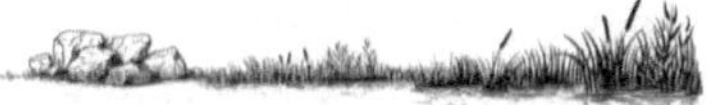

Gad—Good Fortune

Leah, not to be outdone by her sister, decided to also throw her slave, Zilpah, into the childbearing ring.

> When Leah saw that she had stopped having children, she took her slave Zilpah and gave her to Jacob as a wife. And Leah's slave Zilpah bore Jacob a son. Then Leah said, "How fortunate!" So she named him Gad. (Genesis 30:9–11 NASB)

I used to have a trusty old 2001 Ford Taurus I affectionately named Adebisi. Don't ask me why. By the fall of 2012, Adebisi was starting to fail me regularly. It was time to bid him farewell and look for a new vehicle. In the meantime, while I was shopping for a car, my cousin offered me the use of one of his cars, so I could take my time shopping and not feel pressured to make a decision right away. That was awesome until I ran into another car one morning while pulling out of the alley. Fortunately, no one was severely injured, but my borrowed car was ruined. Yeah, I crashed my cousin's car!

This unfortunate turn of events kicked my car shopping plans into high gear. I called my brother, who lived three hours away, to see if he could help me with car shopping. I took the 6:00 a.m. Amtrak from Chicago to Milwaukee one morning. During my 1.5-hour train ride, I was praying, asking God to lead us to the right car and the right salesperson (preferably someone I could identify as a follower of Jesus Christ).

My brother was right on time. I saw him as soon as I walked out of the station, and we got to it. The first dealership did not have what I was looking for, nor the second. The third dealership seemed promising, but the answer was clearly no after test-driving the car and reading the Car Fax report. I was discouraged. My brother, who is always hungry, not surprisingly suggested we take a lunch break. While we ate, he pulled out his iPad and started scouring online for the make and model I was looking for within our radius.

By the time we had finished lunch, he had found one. With stomachs full and hope restored, we got in his car and made our way to the dealership while I was feverishly praying that the car would still be there. My hope went up another level when we saw the car as we pulled into the lot.

We parked and hurriedly made our way toward it; a salesman came out as we peered through the windows. The car was a beautiful black-on-black Mercury Milan with a sunroof, and it looked like it was in pristine condition. We made pleasantries, and he invited us to take the car for a test drive. As I drove the car, I liked it—no, I loved it. But you know, I couldn't tip my hand to the salesman because it was time to negotiate. As I drove back to the dealership, I was rehearsing my negotiating strategy in my head.

When we arrived, the salesman ushered us into his office, and the first thing I saw was a massive Bible on his desk! Now you know, I took this as a sign from God! He stepped out briefly, and my brother took the opportunity to give me some last-minute negotiation coaching. When the salesman returned, I thought, "Put me in, Coach. I'm ready." We went back and forth until we arrived at the price I was shooting for. I was proud of myself, and so was my brother.

The next step was applying for a loan in the finance office. After I paid the down payment and submitted my loan application, which was approved, the finance guy told me a story. He said someone had tried to buy that very car three days ago, but their financing didn't go through. They had said they would return with a bigger down payment but did not. I looked at that man, and with all my confidence in Christ, I said, "That's because God set this car aside for me." All he could do was smile and nod. This, my friend, was good fortune!

P.S. Remember my brother in Rueben, Memorial Stone 1? Well, this is him all grown up.

Recall a time you received an answer from the Lord as "good fortune."

What was happening in your life at that time?

Why did you think of that answer as good fortune?

What was the answer to that prayer? Today, do you regard that answer as good fortune? If so, why?

MEMORIAL STONE 7

Asher—Happy

Leah's slave, Zilpah, did not stop at birthing one son. She became pregnant again, giving Jacob his seventh son, Asher.

> And Leah's slave Zilpah bore Jacob a second
> son. Then Leah said, "Happy am I! For women
> will call me happy." So she named him Asher.
> (Genesis 30:12–13 NASB)

Remember in Napthali, Memorial Stone 5, I told you about how God led me to quit my job and rest? How long would you imagine that time of rest would have been? I imagined three months, six at the most. Well, friend, that time lasted two years and four months. That's right, a whole two years and four months. The details of that season could be an entire book, but I will give you an overview that landed me at this memorial stone.

A few months before I was drawing toward the end of that season, which I now call my Sabbath season, I started getting the sense to prepare myself to start job hunting again. I signed up for a couple of job-search boot camps and started churning out job applications, giving my resume to whomever would take it. But application after application after application, I did not receive any responses.

Weeks later, I was at a friend's house for a Christmas gathering. After mingling and catching up, I made my way to the kitchen sink to do the dishes and give myself some space. (And all of my fellow introverts said amen; sometimes we'd rather do the dishes than have one more conversation). My quiet reprieve was short-lived, as an acquaintance came over to chat and get to know me. I shared about my Sabbath season and what I had learned about myself, as God had revealed my identity in Him, which helped me identify the type of work I was suited for. It was a lovely conversation that I did not think much of other than it being pleasant.

The disappointment in job hunting continued with each lack of response or rejection. A friend even submitted my resume to her company, certain they would hire me, and they said, "No, thank you!" At this point, you are probably wondering, "Girl, what was wrong with your resume?"

Another eight weeks went by without any interviews at all. I was incredibly frustrated and getting angry with God. Then one day, as I cried out to Him again with great frustration, I said, "Please, please, please open the door to a job!" Half an hour after that prayer, I checked my email to find a message from the acquaintance I had met at the Christmas gathering. She was inquiring if I would be interested in a new job opening at her organization. She thought I would be a good fit, given what I had shared with her over a sink full of dishes.

I looked up and said to God, "I am going to apply for this job unless You stop me." I submitted my resume and got a response to schedule an interview within minutes. My first interview was a few days later. It was rigorous, lasting over three hours with a panel of five directors. I was thoroughly interrogated about my two-year employment gap and why I had exited a seventeen-year career.

After the panel interview, I participated in interviews with each director. I thought the first interview would have done it, but they were unsatisfied. I was called in again and asked the same questions from the first interview. While that was frustrating, I had a certain peace knowing this job was mine, no matter how many hoops they made me jump through. They hired me about two and a half weeks after applying for the job. As God would have it, I got the call for the job offer on my birthday!

When I started that job, I finally felt like I was doing work that utilized my gifts and made a greater difference with the people I impacted daily. This job spoke directly to what I was built for and all the areas I thrive in. I was truly happy with this job!

Recall a time you were truly happy.

What was happening in your life at that time?

What was the event that caused you so much happiness? How long had it been since you had started contending for happiness in that area of your life?

MEMORIAL STONE 8

Issachar–There Is Recompense

Zilpah, Leah's slave, not only bore Jacob two sons but also conceived a third time, giving birth to Issachar. In the battle of the babies, Rachel could not keep up and became terribly discouraged. Then Leah's son found the mandrake plants. In biblical times, people prized mandrake plants for their aphrodisiac powers and believed they cured infertility. In desperation, Rachel coveted those plants. So she struck a bargain with her sister.

Leah agreed to provide Rachel with the mandrakes if she allowed Jacob to sleep with Leah that night. Rachel agreed, and when Jacob went to Leah's that night, she gave him her slave to sleep with.

> Then Leah said, "God has given me my reward, because I gave my slave to my husband." So she named him Issachar. (Genesis 30:18 NASB)

In Memorial Stone 7, I was happy! Happy with the work I was doing to impact the world meaningfully. I knew God had led me into this job, but it also came with stretching my faith in my salary. The salary was slightly more than half of my previous salary. There was no way I could cover my mortgage and essential bills with this salary, let alone savings. I asked the Lord, "Do You want me to accept this salary?"

He said yes, so I did. Then I told Him, "It's up to You to cover my bills. I am not going to worry about it." Remember when I said that the details of my Sabbath season could fill an entire book? Well, the following story I am about to share is one of the faith-stretching experiences of that season.

Real talk, my emergency savings did not cover two years and four months of bills. There came a point where I ran dry, and I could not pay my mortgage, among other bills. Can you imagine? I am following the leading of the Lord, and now I cannot pay my mortgage. I called the mortgage company, and they graciously put me on a forbearance plan with a minimum monthly payment. Part of the agreement was to let them know that as soon as I had a regular income again, my regular payments would resume.

To honor that agreement, I called them after securing my job, and they took me off the forbearance plan. But, friends, the salary I had been offered and told to accept by God did not cover my mortgage and essential bills. I also had to refinance by this time because I had missed so many payments that I could not make up in a lump sum.

I applied for refinancing and submitted all of my paperwork with the faith that I would be approved and the numbers would return in my favor. After all, I had been obedient to the Lord's leading.

A few weeks later, I called the mortgage company to make a good faith small payment. After the representative had processed my payment, he gleefully told me that my application was denied and I would have to make at least 3 percent more income to qualify for refinancing. Then he hung up the phone! My jaw dropped. I did not know what to do other than fall to my knees and remind God that this was His idea. So He needed to get me out of it.

I called a friend and processed these events with her. She suggested that I talk to my new boss, tell her the situation, and see if she would give me a raise. After we got off the phone, I asked the Lord if that was the route I should take, and He swiftly responded, "Stop meddling!"

So I stopped but reminded Him day after day of His promise. In the meantime, the mortgage company started processing foreclosure proceedings. I received a legal notice stating my house would be auctioned off in four months. I put that notice on my coffee table and daily told the Lord, "You promised I would not lose my house. I am standing on that promise."

One day, nine weeks after I started my new job, my boss called me to her office. I thought for sure I was in trouble for something. But my boss started telling me a story about how God leads her in her decision-making. I thought, *Cool, but what does this have to do with me?* She followed this up with how pleased she'd been with the work I'd been doing, concluding that she'd like to give me a promotion and a raise. She gave me the paperwork to sign, and my jaw dropped—the raise was 26 percent! I was doing cartwheels in my head because it was more than enough to qualify for refinancing!

I took that paperwork, signed it, and made copies, and as soon as I got home that night, I reapplied for my mortgage refinancing. Several weeks later, I was approved, and the bank stopped the foreclosure proceedings one month before the auction.

Friends, if that's not recompense, I don't know what is! The Lord had seen fit to reward me for my steps of obedience even when He led me into the wilderness. It wasn't an easy journey, but He was faithful to bring recompense.

Definition: *Recompense*—an equivalent or a return for something done, suffered, or given.[1]

---

[1] "Recompense Definition and Meaning," *Merriam-Webster*, accessed 12 Feb, 2024, www.merriam-webster.com/dictionary/recompense.

Recall a time you received recompense.

What was happening in your life at that time? What had you suffered through?

What was the recompense for? And what past event was recompense in response to?

MEMORIAL STONE 9

Zebulan—Honored or Exalted

Now it was Leah's turn again. She conceived and bore Jacob, a sixth son.

> And Leah conceived again and bore a sixth son to Jacob. Then Leah said, "God has endowed me with a good gift; finally my husband will acknowledge me *as his wife*, because I have borne him six sons." So she named him Zebulun."
> (Genesis 30:19–20 NASB)

In my first draft of writing this devotional, I could not pinpoint a time I had felt honored, exalted, or acknowledged in my position. I wrote that in this space. It is all good if you arrive at some of the memorial stones and think, "I have not seen one of these miracles." I trust that you will eventually experience a miracle in that area because that, my friend, is what happened to me.

Two weeks after I had written that I had nothing, I had an experience where I felt honored, exalted, and acknowledged in my position for the very first time in my life. Remember that job that made me happy? The one God had opened the door to after my Sabbath season? Well, at this point, I had been there for four years. I truly loved the work I was doing and the team that I worked with. Then one day, while praying, I heard a still whisper, "Prepare to leave your job."

I kept praying because I wanted to be sure I heard correctly. After several weeks of prayer, I was confident I needed to submit my resignation. (I will share more about this process in Memorial Stone 11.) Once again, I was leaving my job without any prospects. Resigning from a position I had enjoyed and a team I loved dearly was difficult, but I learned over the years that obedience was the better choice.

On my last day of work, my co-workers planned a small going-away celebration for me. Everyone gathered together, there was a beautiful spread of Indian food, and my boss and coworkers said some lovely things about me. Then my boss asked the chairman of the board of directors to pray for me. He told me to sit down in a chair so he could pray a blessing over me.

I sat down, and what I had not anticipated happened. Everyone gathered around me, laying hands on me, as the chairman led in a prayer of blessing over me. As I sat in that chair, I heard a whisper from God. He said, "I wanted you to leave with their blessing." I felt God's feathery light whispers settle on me as my coworkers circled me, laid hands on me, and blessed me. I embraced the shift in my spirit, and their heartfelt sendoff reduced me to tears. I felt honored for the first time. A moment I will never forget.

Recall a time you felt honored and acknowledged in your position.

What was happening in your life at that time?

How were you honored and acknowledged? What event was the honor in response to?

MEMORIAL STONE 10

Benjamin—Son (Daughter) of the Right Hand

We are skipping ahead to Rachel's second pregnancy. (When we get to the bonus memorial stones, we will backtrack to Rachel's first pregnancy.) This pregnancy happened after they had left Laban and were traveling back to the land where Jacob was from.

Unfortunately, Rachel endured arduous labor, managed to name her son, and died shortly after birth. She named him Ben-oni, which means "son of my sorrow," but his father renamed him Benjamin (son of the right hand).

> Then they journeyed on from Bethel; but when there was still some distance to go to Ephrath, Rachel began to give birth and she suffered severe difficulties in her labor. And when she was suffering severe difficulties in her labor, the midwife said to her, "Do not fear, for you have another son!" And it came about, as her soul was departing (for she died), that she named him Ben-oni; but his father called him Benjamin." (Genesis 35:16–18 NASB)

As I mentioned earlier, I seriously thought it would only be a few months of unemployment when I started my Sabbath season. In fact, I fought it for a while. I had been so used to working long hours for seventeen years, so what on earth would I do with all this time? I decided to explore all the parks I could in the area. I would pull up Google Maps, find a park, and drive there. As you can imagine, this got old fairly quickly. Some days, I just sat and sulked at God in my house. That didn't last too long either.

Then one day, a friend sent me a sermon from a church named Expression58. The sermon outlined how to discern the voice of God. Pastor Jen Toledo pointed out we hear three voices that we need to learn to differentiate: our own voice, the voice of the enemy, and the voice of God. She also spoke about the importance of knowing our identity in Christ, which is integral to learning to discern the voice of God. That sermon was a turning point for me. I finished the sermon series and hungrily sought out sermons related to hearing the voice of God and/or our identity.

I found myself tuning into live streams of Expression58 soaking up their teachings rooted in identity. After listening, I would pour into my Bible, highlighting, taking notes, and praying about what I was learning. God gave me a handful of friends whom I would talk to regularly, and we would share with one another what God was speaking to us through Scripture, sermons, songs, and life lessons. The more I dove in, the more I realized that I was shedding the identity I had taken on in my career. I had been so tied to what I did that it became who I was. This time of immersion taught me my career was something I did, not who I was.

This time set my foundation, cementing my identity in Christ and growing my trust in Him. I slowly started to see myself as a daughter, His daughter. I stopped seeing Him as the angry Father in the sky waiting to punish me and started to see Him as a doting Father. The more I saw myself as a daughter of the loving Father, the more I could trust Him to provide for me. By the end of my Sabbath season, I finally *knew* that I was the daughter of the right hand.

Recall when you became aware you were the daughter or son of the right hand.

What was happening in your life at that time?

What event made you realized that you are the daughter or son of the right hand? And what does that mean to you, to be the daughter or son of the right hand?

MEMORIAL STONE 11

Manasseh—Causes Me to Forget

Stepping out of the Leah versus Rachel childbearing ring for the moment, this next memorial stone will discuss healing from difficult seasons. Let's focus on Jacob's favorite son, Joseph, for the moment.

Fast forwarding through the story, Joseph's brothers sold him into slavery and told their father, Jacob, that wild animals killed him. This started a long chain of events that eventually led to Joseph becoming second in command to the Pharaoh in Egypt. (For more details read Genesis chapters 37–46. It's a fascinating illustration of how God works behind the scenes in our lives, giving beauty for ashes.) In chapter 41, Joseph's wife, Asenath, gave birth to their first son, Manasseh.

> Joseph named the firstborn Manasseh; "For," *he said*, "God has made me forget all my trouble and all of my father's household." (Genesis 41:51 NASB)

What does it mean to forget? We don't necessarily forget the difficult seasons, but we can get to a place of healing where the pain is no longer recalled when a memory comes up. In Simeon, Memorial Stone 2, I tell the story of my father seeing me and walking away from me. That experience devastated me, consequently shaping how I related to God the Father and the men in my life. At that moment,

I decided I could never fully trust a father and, by extension, men. I learned that they all eventually walk away and are unreliable.

I carried this belief into adulthood, and as I look back, I see how it affected my relationships with men. When my ex-husband and I were dating, one day, we had our first major argument. He left my apartment, and my expectation was that he would not come back. Well, he did come back, and I was surprised. In fact, I said to him, "I didn't think you would come back."

He asked why not, and I just shrugged. Unfortunately, several years later after we got married, he did leave for good. This once again further cemented my belief that men leave.

As I write this section, it is May 2023, and it wasn't until three months ago that this father's wound was healed. My healing came through an Exchange ministry session, which is a discipleship model developed by Becky Castle purposed to restore the conversations between God and man. The session is a "facilitator-led conversation between the [recipient] and the Lord to discover His truth for [their] life." (Castle 2021, 203) The foundation for this ministry stems from Romans 1:25 (NASB), which states:

> For they exchanged the truth of God for
> falsehood, and worshiped and served the creature
> rather than the Creator, who is blessed forever.
> Amen.

In the Exchange ministry, we exchange ingrained lies we have believed (often since childhood) for the truth of God about specific painful situations in our lives. These lies are "stuck places" described by Castle in her book:

> Throughout our lives, we've stored within
> us thousands of experiences, often not knowing
> what's going to trigger something in us or how
> we'll cope. All along the way, we each have God's
> embedded blueprint of needing deep commu-
> nion and intimacy with Him, so we start to feel

frustrated, sad, hopeless, and lonely, bumping into our lack over and over. At some point, our coping stops benefitting us, and our triggers stop us from being able to move through life. We call that a "stuck place." Some people describe the feeling as "hitting a wall in life."

Our current "stuck places" are rooted in a lie that we believed when we experienced a painful place of lack…. The key to the Exchange is this: wherever there is a lack of revelation in me to understand the goodness and righteousness of God, it is because I believe a lie. (Castle 2021,12, 14).

Well, apparently, I had hit a wall in my relationship with God as Father, which landed me in my ministry session on February 10, 2023. One day in December 2022 during my time of prayer, I heard a whisper from the Lord, "Prepare to leave your job." This surprised me, but I asked what I needed to do next to which He responded, "Watch and listen." I went about normal life until a series of events triggered the memory of my conversation with God. In January 2023, my career began shifting, causing me to pray intentionally about leaving the God-given job I mentioned in "Memorial Stone 7: Happy." After seeking and praying and seeking and praying, I still didn't have clarity from God about what He wanted me to do. I felt incredibly frustrated and did not understand why I could not hear from God. My alliance shifted, and I was no longer invested in either staying or leaving my job, recognizing what God wanted me to do became my sole desire. Discouraged, I signed up for my Exchange session to tackle the question of resignation.

As we settled into the session, the memory of my father walking away from me in childhood quickly surfaced. Through the session, I realized the decisions I made at that moment of my abandonment by my father now affected and distorted my ability to trust God in this next big decision I needed to make. The "want" to follow Him was there, but the trust was not. Once God revealed the lie, I repented, forgave my earthly father, and invited God to heal this deep wound. God showed me in that session how, when my father abandoned me, He stepped in, took my hand, and took his place. I had not been aware of it until that moment. At the end of the session, I realized I needed that place healed in my heart so I could move forward on a new journey of faith with God. A journey that could not be embarked on with only partial trust.

The healing of this wound and the redemptive action from the Father caused me to "forget" the pain of that event. This also began a new leg of my journey with God, requiring, and giving me, a new level of trust in Him.

I harbor no unforgiveness toward my father. I understand now that he was a broken man who did not know how to love. I, on the other hand, am now a stronger woman, more deeply rooted in my trust in God, embracing faith, and excited to step into the unknown with Him, and this is all because I eliminated the lie and stepped into God's truth.

To learn more about the Exchange ministry and/or sign up for a session, visit Theexchangecenter.org. In addition, I highly recommend Becky Castle's book *The Exchange: Surrender to the Process*, available for purchase at Launchstore.org.

Recall a time you realized you had forgotten about a troubling event in your life.

What was happening in your life at that time? Who do you need to forgive to help you transition to a place of forgetting?

What events led you to forget this troubling event in your life?

MEMORIAL STONE 12

Ephraim—Doubly Fruitful

I need to take a moment here and give you the backstory before we discuss the next memorial stone. In Genesis chapter 48 (seriously this is such a good story) Joseph's father Jacob claimed his first two sons, Manasseh and Ephraim as his own. This allowed Jacob to bestow great honors on Joseph's children, which eventually manifested into the half tribes of Manasseh and Ephraim (one of the twelve tribes of Israel). In the Bible, the Jews believed that their father's final blessing before he died carried the most weight. The blessings received from their fathers were more important than any material item and they believed these blessings prophesied their entire family's future. In short, each child prayed for a favorable blessing.

Now, back to how Ephraim is doubly fruitful. Asenath, gave Joseph a second son, Ephraim. Ephraim means "fruitful in the land of affliction."

> And he named the second son Ephraim;
> "For," *he said,* "God has made me fruitful in the
> land of my affliction." (Genesis 41:52 NASB)

Eventually, in Genesis chapter 48, even though Ephraim is the second child, God led Jacob to give the blessing of the oldest child to him meaning he became doubly blessed. The blessing is beautiful and tender, so I am including it here.

> When Israel saw Joseph's sons, he said, "Who are these?" And Joseph said to his father, "They are my sons, whom God has given me here." So he said, "Bring them to me, please, so that I may bless them." Now the eyes of Israel were *so* dim from age *that* he could not see. And Joseph brought them close to him, and he kissed them and embraced them. And Israel said to Joseph, "I never expected to see your face, and behold, God has let me see your children as well!" Then Joseph took them from his knees, and bowed with his face to the ground. And Joseph took them both, Ephraim with his right hand toward Israel's left, and Manasseh with his left hand toward Israel's right, and brought them close to him. But Israel reached out his right hand and placed it on the head of Ephraim, who was the younger, and his left hand on Manasseh's head, crossing his hands, although Manasseh was the firstborn. And he blessed Joseph, and said,
> "The God before whom my fathers Abraham and Isaac walked,
> The God who has been my shepherd all my life to this day,
> The angel who has redeemed me from all evil,
> Bless the boys;
> And may my name live on in them,
> And the names of my fathers Abraham and Isaac;
> And may they grow into a multitude in the midst of the earth."
> When Joseph saw that his father placed his right hand on Ephraim's head, it displeased him;

and he grasped his father's hand to move it from Ephraim's head to Manasseh's head. And Joseph said to his father, "Not so, my father, for this one is the firstborn. Place your right hand on his head." But his father refused and said, "I know, my son, I know; he also will become a people and he also will be great. However, his younger brother shall be greater than he, and his descendants shall become a multitude of nations." So he blessed them that day, saying,

"By you Israel will pronounce blessing, saying,

'May God make you like Ephraim and Manasseh!'"

And *so* he put Ephraim before Manasseh. (Genesis 48:8–20 NASB)

This memorial stone culminates the entire purpose of this devotional journal. Each of these memorial stones is evidence of God working in my life and yours. Throughout this journal, you have been mining God's beautiful memorial stones and recording how he has shown up, ordered your steps, and giving you beauty for ashes. This is where I want you to realize God cherishes you and loves you. You are doubly fruitful. He created you for such a time as this.

I am doubly fruitful because He saw and led me through the land of affliction in the different seasons of my life. Each one of my miracles grew from painful, difficult, impossible, scary, you-name-it situations. Recognizing God's grace and miracle in each situation is evidence of the fruitfulness of the affliction. So here is what I know for sure:

- My Father sees me.
- He hears me.
- I praise Him.
- He vindicates me.
- I wrestle.

- He gives me good fortune.
- He makes me happy.
- He gives me recompense.
- He honors me.
- He calls me daughter.
- He allows me to forget and heals me.
- I am doubly fruitful!

Recall when you realized God made you fruitful in the "land of your affliction."

What was happening in your life at that time?

What fruit did you harvest in this place of affliction?

Review each previously recorded memorial stone and take a moment to thank God for your miracles.

BONUS MEMORIAL STONES

In this section, I note Levi and Joseph as "bonus memorial stones." While a tribe, God set aside the Levites as the holy priests as their reward for not worshiping the calf of gold in the wilderness during their exodus from Egypt. Because God became their portion, they did not need to inherit land in the promised land.

Reuben, Jacob's first son, lost his birthright when he sinned against his father by sleeping with his concubine. As a result, Joseph received the eldest child's "double portion" opening the door for his sons, Manasseh and Ephraim, to become their own half tribes of Israel.

Levi—Attached

Levi was Jacob's third son, born by Leah. At this point, she had borne three sons in a row and was still hoping that her husband's feelings toward her would change.

> And she conceived again and gave birth to a son, and said, "Now this time my husband will become attached to me, because I have borne him three sons." Therefore he was named Levi. (Genesis 29:34 NASB)

I am a member of the national organization 4word. My local chapter holds weekly Bible studies. Recently, we completed the book *Restore—Remembering Life's Hurts with the God who Rebuilds* by Susannah Baker. This book hypothesizes that each person has what she termed as an "attachment style."

> Every human is born wired to be securely attached to the people in their lives, usually to their parents first. This relationship sets up the child for how they will attach to other people… Research shows that the way you attach to your primary caretaker predicts with 80% accuracy how you will attach to every other person in your life as well. Simply put, how you attach to your

> parents or primary caretaker in those foundational years of life tells you how you will form attachments to others for the rest of your life—attachments to your spouse, your own children, your friends, your co-workers, your acquaintances, and most importantly, to God. (Baker 2022, 12–13)

Identifying your personal attachment style will help you with this memorial stone.

I learned there is one secure attachment style and three insecure attachment styles: Secure Attachment, Insecure-Avoidant Attachment, Insecure-Ambivalent Attachment, and Insecure-Disorganized Attachment. Baker referenced the research from Dr. Gregg Jantz to pose the following questions to determine each person's attachment style:

- "Am I worthy of being loved?"
- "Am I able to do what I need to do to get the love I need?"
- "Are other people reliable and trustworthy?"
- "Are other people accessible and willing to respond to me when I need them?" (Baker 2022, 32)

Baker goes on to define each attachment style with the answers to the above questions.

Adults with secure attachment

Securely attached adults answer the four questions in this way:

- "Yes, I am worthy of being loved."
- "Yes, I am able to do what I need to do to get the love I need."

- "Yes, other people are reliable and trustworthy."
- "Yes, other people are accessible and willing to respond to me when I need them." (Baker 2022, 33)

Adults with insecure-avoidant attachment

Insecure-avoidant attached adults answer the four questions in this way:

- "I am worthy of being loved not for who I am but for what I can do."
- "I am able to do what I need to do to get the love I need because I give it to myself."
- "No, other people are not reliable and trustworthy, so I need to rely only on myself."
- "No, other people are not accessible and willing to respond to me when I need them, so I need to take care of myself." (Baker 2022, 34)

Adults with insecure-ambivalent attachment

Insecure-ambivalent attached adults answer the four questions in this way:

- "Sometimes I am worthy of being loved and sometimes I'm not. I am constantly working to secure other people's love and approval."
- "I am always afraid others will leave or abandon me and that my needs will not be met."
- "It's very hard for me to trust that other people are reliable and trustworthy; it is very hard for me to even trust myself."

- "No, other people are not accessible and willing to respond to me when I need them, so I vacillate between attempting to control their responses through my own neediness or anger." (Baker 2022, 36)

Adults with insecure-disorganized attachment

Insecure-disorganized attached adults answer the four questions in this way:

- "No, I am not worthy of being loved."
- "No, I am not able to do what I need to do to get the love I need."
- "No, other people are not reliable and trustworthy."
- "No, other people are not accessible and willing to respond to me when I need them." (Baker 2022, 38)

As I read the answers to each attachment definition, I realized that I exhibited insecure-avoidant attachment in my relationships.

After learning about our insecure attachment style, the book walked us through uncovering and allowing God to heal the places that caused us to develop our specific attachment style so we could heal personally and securely attach to God. This enables us to begin to heal our insecurely attached relationships. Let me give you some context on how this manifested for me personally.

In my Sabbath season, God completely stripped me. He stripped me down career-wise, financially, and even relationally. I could no longer hide behind my career title. For the first time, I had a blank slate for a schedule. I had drained every ounce of my savings. The cherry on top? Because of my transfer, I lived in a new city far from my family and close friends. My only option was God. In Benjamin - Memorial Stone 10, I detail how I deepened my relationship with God. By the end of this study, I realized that during my Sabbath season, I learned to securely attach to God and still am, working on healing each of my other insecurely attached relationships.

The book gave me the language I needed, and as I look at this memorial stone, I realize the significant stripping God led me through enabled me to become attached to my heavenly Father. While God has always been attached to me, I am now confident that I am securely attached to Him.

Recall when you remember the Lord gave you a blessing that you thought would cause something or someone else to become attached to you.

What was happening in your life at that time?

What was the person or thing you were hoping to attach to you?

What blessing did the Lord give you that caused you to expect attachment from that person or thing? What was your ultimate realization about this blessing?

MEMORIAL STONE 14

Joseph—Jehovah Has Added

Joseph was Rachel's first son and Jacob's eleventh. God finally rolled away the reproach of childlessness from Rachel when she conceived Joseph. Because of his love for Rachel, Joseph became Jacob's favorite son. He became his "Jehovah Has Added."

> Then God remembered Rachel, and God listened to her and opened her womb. So she conceived and gave birth to a son, and said, "God has taken away my disgrace." And she named him Joseph, saying, "May the LORD give me another son." (Genesis 30:22–24)

At 8:30 p.m. on Monday, August 13, 2012, Mum died after a six-year battle with cancer. I was by her side that evening along with my dear sister-friend and roommate Chaustine, my aunt Rose, and Dina, Mum's hospice nurse. My journal entry from that evening reads, "Mama passed today at about 8:30 p.m. She just slowly stopped breathing. It's sad to know I'll never see her in the flesh again, but I'm happy she's with her heavenly Father. The place she has always wanted to be. I feel at peace and joyful that she is where she has always wanted to be."

Looking back and reading that journal entry, I am so clear that the peace of God in me that surpasses all understanding wrote that. Not me.

A few days later, on Friday, August 17, we gathered friends and family and buried Mum in Chicago. Several of us spoke at her service, including Reverend Green, who came to know Mum in her last days. He said, "I suspect Irene never prayed for an easy life because if she had, God would have answered her prayer given the way she prayed." Even on her death bed, Mum would always end each visit from Rev. Green by praying *for* him. I recorded his statement in my journal and began walking down a road of wondering what exactly Mum had prayed for.

My wanderings led me to ask what exactly Irene Savanhu's legacy was. What legacy had she left behind?

Legacy is defined as the following:

1. a gift by will especially of money or other property.
2. something transmitted by or received from an ancestor or predecessor or from the past person's life.[2]

There was no financial or property inheritance which left the second definition. What was the long-lasting impact that my mother had? I had no idea. Was it raising three children? If so, was that enough? I honestly had no idea, and this had me spiraling! Did Mum die without fulfilling her purpose?

These questions consumed me day in and day out. I would spend hours pondering them until I would drive myself crazy, then I'd repeat the process over and over and over again. I felt like Rachel in that the reproach upon my life was that my mother died without a purpose-filled life. What if the same happened to me?

Up until that point, my life seemed pointless. It seemed like I ran into more obstacles than I did clear roads. I would often take two steps forward and ten steps back. Sure, I had a great family, friends, and a decent life, but I was nowhere near where I thought I should be. Would my life be purposeless, like I had wrongly perceived my mother's to be? This crisis of purpose went on for two whole years.

---

[2] "Legacy Definition and Meaning," *Merriam-Webster*, accessed 12 Feb, 2024, www.merriam-webster.com /dictionary/legacy."

There were ebbs and flows. Sometimes it seemed better; other times, it seemed worse. But along the way, God kept giving me nuggets.

The first nugget was through a women's conference speaker. She spoke about the legacy of faith her grandmother had modeled, and as she shared, I heard a whisper in my spirit, "Your Mum left a legacy of faith."

The second nugget was from my spiritual mentor, Millie. She was praying for me one day and said I would receive my mother's mantle. I had no idea what she was talking about, so I did not give it much thought until several weeks later as I sat on the side of my bed praying out loud. I heard myself praying exactly the way I heard Mum pray when I would get up to get ready for work at 4:00 a.m. And I thought, *Oh wow, so this is the mantle Millie spoke about.*

Finally, in June 2014, I decided to deal with the issue head-on and signed up for a Sozo inner healing session. Sozo inner healing is described as the following on bethelsozo.com:

> Sozo is NOT counseling. It's a gentle, yet powerful, tool for inner healing and deliverance.
> Goal: Uncover and address root issues that hinder your personal growth and relationship with God and others.

My burning question for my Sozo session was, "Did Mum fulfill her calling while she was here on earth?" During the session, as I leaned into the voice of the Father, Son, and Holy Spirit, I received confirmation after confirmation that she had fulfilled her purpose and that, above all, she had left a legacy of faith. These answers also helped answer the questions about the purpose of my life. I knew then that, if nothing else, my purpose would be to perpetuate the legacy of faith Mum had left behind.

Jehovah added, or revealed, the foundational purpose of my life: to be a person of faith. The reproach I put upon myself and my mother rolled away. Over the years, God continued to remove layers from me that further define the areas I am purposed to step into. Still, governing it all is the foundation of faith He put beneath me to travel this adventurous and sometimes scary journey with Him.

Recall when you realized that Jehovah rolled away reproach and added onto you.

What was happening in your life at that time?

What did Jehovah add to you? Why was this a blessing to you?

CONCLUSION

You did it! Give yourself a round of applause! Give a shout of praise for the miracles of the Lord! He is good! He is faithful! He loves unconditionally!

Lastly, I will leave you with this little passage I came across at a silent-centering prayer retreat. It fits the work you have just completed as you journeyed through this book.

I couldn't find the exact source of the quote, but the handout noted that it was from the Sayings of the Desert Fathers:

> Last evening my dog saw a rabbit running for cover among the bushes of the desert and he began to chase the rabbit, barking loudly. Soon other dogs joined in the chase, and they were barking and running as well. They ran a great distance and alerted many other dogs. Soon the desert was echoing the sounds of their pursuit but the chase went on into the night.
>
> After a little while, many of the dogs grew tired and dropped out. A few chased the rabbit until the night was nearly spent. By morning, only my dog continued the hunt. "Do you understand," the old man said, "what I have told you?"
>
> "No," replied the young monk. "Please tell me, father."

"It is simple," said the desert father. "My dog saw the rabbit."

This passage struck me because you have documented evidence of you having seen the "rabbit" and continuing the chase. Once we experience God or realize that we have experienced Him, we are drawn to Him like a moth to the fire. We continuously seek Him.

As you have read in my own experiences and, I am sure, yours, our faith journeys often look foolish to the world. Sometimes, if you are like me, you wonder if you are foolish. But after having seen the hand of the Lord on my life, your life; after having felt the wind of the Holy Spirit blow through; and after having felt the weight of the Father's love, I, you, have seen the "rabbit" and will continue to tirelessly chase after His goodness, His mercy, His love, His leading.

I could go on and on and on. What I know for sure is that even in the difficulties of my journey, He has never left me nor forsaken me.

Keep chasing, friends. Keep chasing.

Now that you have walked through each memorial stone and detailed the events around it, take a moment to summarize your miracles and memorial stones. Use these as regular living reminders of God's love and goodness for you.

I encourage you to be creative and devise your own method of summarization or simply scan the QR code below to download the worksheets I created.

These first twelve plus two memorial stones are just your beginning, your foundation. As you continue your journey with the Lord, stay in the habit of documenting your memorial stones so you can celebrate how the Lord moves in your life.

Blessings + miracles.

—Brenda

Go to inspiredmusing.com/memorialstones

REFERENCES

Baker, Susannah. 2022. *Restore: Remembering Life's Hurts with the God Who Rebuilds*. ISBN 978-1-7379589-1-8.
Castle, Becky. 2021. *The Exchange: Surrender to the Process*. Texas: Lucid Books. ISBN 978-1-63296-461-8.

Brenda Savanhu is a vision strategist, founder of Inspired Musing Consulting, cohost of *Habits & Stones Podcast*, and author of *Memorial Stones: A Guided Devotional Journal of Foundational Miracles in Your Life*. The formative years of Brenda's childhood began in London, England, and rounded off in Bulawayo, Zimbabwe. An avid reader, she always traveled with a book in her hand as a child. Using the written word to escape, she delved into the world of Nancy Drew or the deductive genius of Hercule Poirot in Agatha Christie's novels.

In the latter part of her childhood, Brenda's cousin introduced her to the Christian faith, but she did not grow to fully own her faith until adulthood. The United States of America is now her home since she earned a full academic scholarship and moved to Wisconsin to attend university at the age of eighteen. Brenda lives and works out of her home in Houston, Texas. She is actively involved in her church community, still loves to read, and will travel whenever the opportunity presents itself.

Connect with Brenda on Habits & Stones, a podcast she co-hosts with her friend Wendy Wall, author of *The Holy Habit*. Drop in on their conversations about their books, faith journeys, and intimacy with God. Check out her website to download free resources, and follow her on social media for more.

www.inspiredmusing.com
www.habitsandstones.com

Instagram and Facebook
@brendasavanhu
@habitsandstones
@inspiredmusing

www.ingramcontent.com/pod-product-compliance
Lightning Source LLC
Chambersburg PA
CBHW031413160726
47993CB00003B/1209